CONVENTION BETWEEN THE   GOVERNMENT OF THE UNITED STATES
OF AMERICA AND THE GOVERNMENT OF THE PEOPLE'S REPUBLIC
OF BANGLADESH FOR THE AVOIDANCE OF DOUBLE TAXATION AND THE
PREVENTION OF FISCAL EVASION WITH RESPECT TO TAXES ON INCOME

CONVENTION BETWEEN THE   GOVERNMENT OF THE UNITED STATES
OF AMERICA AND THE GOVERNMENT OF THE PEOPLE'S REPUBLIC
OF BANGLADESH FOR THE AVOIDANCE OF DOUBLE TAXATION AND THE
PREVENTION OF FISCAL EVASION WITH RESPECT TO TAXES ON INCOME

The Government of the United States of America and the Government of the People's Republic of Bangladesh, desiring to conclude a convention for the avoidance of double taxation and the prevention of fiscal evasion with respect to taxes on income, have agreed as follows:

ARTICLE 1

Personal Scope

1. Except as otherwise provided in this Convention, this Convention shall apply to persons who are residents of one or both of the Contracting States.

2.   a) Notwithstanding any provision of this Convention except paragraph 3 of this Article, a Contracting State may tax its residents (as determined under Article 4 (Fiscal Domicile)), and by reason of citizenship may tax its citizens, as if this Convention had not come into effect.

b) For this purpose, the term "citizen" shall include a former citizen or long-term resident whose loss of such status had as one of its principal purposes the avoidance of tax (as defined under the laws of the Contracting State of which the person was a citizen or long-term resident), but only for a period of 10 years following such loss. The term "long-term resident" shall mean any individual who is a lawful permanent resident of a Contracting State in 8 or more income years or taxable years during the preceding 15 income years or taxable years. In determining whether the threshold in the preceding sentence is met, there shall not count any year in which the individual is treated as a resident of the other   Contracting State under this Convention, or as a resident of any country other than the first-mentioned Contracting State under the provisions of any other tax treaty of that State, and, in either case, the individual does not waive the benefits of such treaty applicable to residents of the other country.

3. The provisions of paragraph 2 shall not affect:

a) the benefits conferred by a Contracting State under paragraph 2 of Article 9 (Associated Enterprises), paragraphs 2 and 5 of Article 19 (Pensions, Et Cetera), Articles 23 (Relief From Double Taxation), 24 (Nondiscrimination), and 25 (Mutual Agreement Procedure); and

b) the benefits conferred by a Contracting State under Articles 20 (Government Service), 21 (Teachers, Students and Trainees) and 27 (Effect of Convention on Diplomatic Agents and Consular Officers, Domestic Laws, And Other Treaties), upon individuals who are neither citizens of, nor have immigrant status in, that State.

ARTICLE 2

Taxes Covered

1. This Convention shall apply to taxes on income imposed by a Contracting State.

2. The existing taxes to which this Convention shall apply are:

a) In the United States: the Federal income taxes imposed by the Internal Revenue Code;

b) In Bangladesh: the income tax (including surcharges calculated by reference to income taxes).

3. The Convention shall apply also to any identical or substantially similar taxes which are imposed by a Contracting State after the date of signature of this Convention in addition

to, or in place of, the existing taxes. The competent authorities of the Contracting States shall notify each other of any changes that have been made in their respective taxation or other laws that significantly affect their obligations under this Convention.

ARTICLE 3
General Definitions

1. For the purposes of this Convention, unless the context otherwise requires:

a) the term "person" includes an individual, a partnership, a company, an estate, a trust, and any other body of persons;

b) the term "company" means any body corporate or any entity which is treated as a body corporate for tax purposes according to the laws of the Contracting State in which it is organized or has its place of effective management;

c) the terms "enterprise of a Contracting State" and "enterprise of the other Contracting State" mean respectively an enterprise carried on by a resident of a Contracting State and an enterprise carried on by a resident of the other Contracting State;

d) the term "international traffic" means any transport by a ship or aircraft, except where such transport is solely between places in a Contracting State;

e) the term "competent authority" means:

i) in the United States: the Secretary of the Treasury or his delegate, and

ii) in Bangladesh: the National Board of Revenue or its authorized representative;

f) the term "United States" means the United States of America, and includes the states thereof and the District of Columbia; such term also includes the territorial sea thereof and the sea bed and subsoil of the submarine areas adjacent to that territorial sea, over which the United States exercises sovereign rights in accordance with international law; the term, however, does not include Puerto Rico, the Virgin Islands, Guam or any other United States possession or territory;

g) the term "Bangladesh" means the People's Republic of Bangladesh; such term also includes the territorial sea thereof and the sea bed and subsoil of the submarine areas adjacent to that territorial sea, over which Bangladesh exercises sovereign rights in accordance with international law;

h) The term "national" means:

i) in relation to the United States, all individuals possessing the citizenship of the United States of America and all legal persons, partnerships and associations deriving their status as such from the laws in force in the United States; and

ii) in relation to Bangladesh, all individuals possessing the nationality of Bangladesh and all legal persons, partnerships and associations deriving their status as such from the laws in force in Bangladesh.

2. As regards the application of this Convention by a Contracting State, any term not defined herein shall, unless the context otherwise requires, or the competent authorities agree to a common meaning pursuant to the provisions of Article 25 (Mutual Agreement Procedure), have the meaning which it has at that time under the laws of that State concerning the taxes to which this Convention applies, any meaning under the applicable tax laws of that State prevailing over a meaning given to the term under other laws of that State.

ARTICLE 4

Fiscal Domicile

1. For purposes of this Convention, the term "resident of a Contracting State" means any person who, under the laws of that State, is liable to tax therein by reason of his domicile, residence, citizenship, place of management, place of incorporation, or any other criterion of a similar nature, and also includes that State and any political subdivision or local authority thereof, provided, however, that:

    a) This term does not include any person who is liable to tax in that State in respect only of income from sources in that State;

    b) An item of income derived through an entity that is a partnership, trust or estate under the laws of either Contracting State shall be considered to be derived by a resident of a Contracting State to the extent that the item is treated for purposes of the taxation law of such Contracting State as the income of a resident, either in its hands or in the hands of its partners or beneficiaries;

    c) A legal person organized under the laws of a Contracting State and that is generally exempt from tax in that State and is established and maintained in that State either:

        i) exclusively for a religious, charitable, educational, scientific, or other similar purpose; or

        ii) to provide pensions or other similar benefits to employees pursuant to a plan

is to be treated for purposes of this paragraph as a resident of that Contracting State.

2. Where by reason of the provisions of paragraph 1 an individual is a resident of both Contracting States, then his status shall be determined as follows:

a) The individual   shall be deemed to be a resident of the State in which he has a permanent home available; if such individual has a permanent home available in both States, or in neither State, he shall be deemed to be a resident of the State with which his personal and economic relations are closer (center of vital interests);

b) If the State in which the individual's center of vital interest cannot be determined, he shall be deemed to be a resident of the State in which he has an habitual abode;

c) If the individual has an habitual abode in both States or in neither of them, he shall be deemed to be a resident of the State of which he is a national; or

d) If the individual is a national of both States or of neither of them, the competent authorities of the Contracting States shall settle the question by mutual agreement.

3. Where by reason of the provisions of paragraph 1 a company is a resident of both Contracting States, then if it is created or organized under the laws of a Contracting State or a political subdivision thereof, it shall be treated as a resident of that State.

4. Where by reason of the provisions of paragraph 1 a person other than an individual or a company is a resident of both Contracting States, the competent authorities of the Contracting States shall endeavor to settle the question by mutual agreement and to determine the mode of application of the Convention to such person.

ARTICLE 5

<u>Permanent Establishment</u>

1. For the purposes of this Convention, the term "permanent establishment" means a fixed place of business through which the business of an enterprise is wholly or partly carried on.

2. The term "permanent establishment" shall include especially:

a) a place of management;

b) a branch;

c) an office;

d) a factory;

e) a workshop;

f) a store or other sales outlet;

g) a warehouse, in relation to a person providing storage facilities for others; and

h) a mine, an oil or gas well, a quarry, or any other place of extraction of natural resources.

3. A building site or construction or installation project, or an installation or drilling rig used for the exploration or development of natural resources, constitutes a permanent establishment only if it lasts more than 183 days.

4. Notwithstanding the preceding provisions of this Article, the term "permanent establishment" shall be deemed not to include:

a) the use of facilities solely for the purpose of storage or display of goods or merchandise belonging to the enterprise;

b) the maintenance of a stock of goods or merchandise belonging to the enterprise solely for the purpose of storage or display;

c) the maintenance of a stock of goods or merchandise belonging to the enterprise solely for the purpose of processing by another enterprise;

d) the maintenance of a fixed place of business solely for the purpose of purchasing goods or merchandise, or of collecting information, for the enterprise;

e) the maintenance of a fixed place of business solely for the purpose of carrying on, for the enterprise, any other activity of a preparatory or auxiliary character;

f) the maintenance of a fixed place of business solely for any combination of activities mentioned in subparagraphs a) to e), provided that the overall activity of the fixed place of business resulting from this combination is of a preparatory or auxiliary character.

5. Notwithstanding the preceding provisions of this Article, the term "permanent establishment" shall be deemed not to include the use of facilities or the maintenance of a stock of goods or merchandise belonging to the enterprise for the purpose of occasional delivery of such goods or merchandise.

6. A person acting in a Contracting State on behalf of an enterprise of the other Contracting State--other than an agent of an independent status to whom paragraph 7 of this Article applies--shall be deemed to be a permanent establishment in the first-mentioned State if:

a) he has, and habitually exercises, in the first-mentioned State, a general authority to conclude contracts on behalf of the enterprise, unless his activities are limited to those described in either paragraph 4 or paragraph 5; or

b) he has no such authority, but habitually maintains in the first-mentioned State a stock of goods or merchandise belonging to the enterprise from which he regularly fills orders or makes deliveries on behalf of the enterprise, and additional activities conducted in that State on behalf of the enterprise have contributed to the conclusion of the sale of such goods or merchandise.

7. An enterprise shall not be deemed to have a permanent establishment in a Contracting State merely because it carries on business in that State through a broker, general commission agent or any other agent of an independent status, provided that such persons are acting in the ordinary course of their business.

8. The fact that a company which is a resident of a Contracting State controls or is controlled by a company which is a resident of the other Contracting State, or which carries on business in that other State (whether through a permanent establishment or otherwise), shall not of itself constitute either company a permanent establishment of the other.

ARTICLE 6

Income From Immovable Property

1. Income derived by a resident of a Contracting State from immovable property (real property), including income from agriculture or forestry, situated in the other Contracting State may be taxed in that other State.

2. The term "immovable property" shall have the meaning which it has under the law of the Contracting State in which the property in question is situated. The term shall in any case include property accessory to immovable property, livestock and equipment used in agriculture, forestry and fishery, rights to which the provisions of general law respecting landed property apply, usufruct of immovable property and rights to variable or fixed payments as consideration for the working of, or the right to work, mineral deposits, sources and other natural resources; ships, boats and aircraft shall not be regarded as immovable property.

3. The provisions of paragraph 1 shall apply to income derived from the direct use, letting, or use in any other form of immovable property.

4. The provisions of paragraphs 1 and 3 shall also apply to the income from immovable property of an enterprise and to income from immovable property used for the performance of independent personal services.

ARTICLE 7

Business Profits

1. The business profits of an enterprise of a Contracting State shall be taxable only in that State unless the enterprise carries on business in the other Contracting State through a permanent establishment situated therein. If the enterprise carries on business as aforesaid, the business profits of the enterprise may be taxed in that other State but only so much of them as is attributable to that permanent establishment.

2. Subject to the provisions of paragraph 3, where an enterprise of a Contracting State carries on business in the other Contracting State through a permanent establishment situated therein, there shall in each Contracting State be attributed to that permanent establishment the business profits which it might be expected to make if it were a distinct and independent enterprise engaged in the same or similar activities under the same or similar conditions.

3. In determining the business profits of a permanent establishment, there shall be allowed as deductions those expenses which are incurred for the purposes of the permanent establishment, including a reasonable allocation of executive and general administrative expenses, research and development expenses, interest, and other expenses incurred for the purposes of the enterprise as a whole or the part thereof which includes the permanent establishment, whether incurred in the State in which the permanent establishment is situated or elsewhere.

4. No business profits shall be attributed to a permanent establishment by reason of the mere purchase by that permanent establishment of goods or merchandise for the enterprise.

5. For the purposes of the preceding paragraphs, the business profits to be attributed to the permanent establishment shall be determined by the same method year by year unless there is good and sufficient reason to the contrary.

6. Where business profits include items of income which are dealt with separately in other Articles of this Convention, then the provisions of those Articles shall not be affected by the provisions of this Article.

7. For the purposes of this Convention, "business profits" means income derived from any trade or business whether carried on by an individual, company, enterprise or any other person, or group of persons, including the rental of tangible personal (movable) property and performance of personal services by an enterprise.

8. For the implementation of paragraphs 1 and 2 of this Article, paragraph 5 of Article 10 (Dividends), paragraph 4 of Article 11 (Interest), paragraph 4 of Article 12 (Royalties), paragraph 2 of Article 13 (Capital Gains), Article 15 (Independent Personal Services) and paragraph 2 of Article 22 (Other Income), any income, gain, or expense attributable to a permanent establishment or fixed base during its existence is taxable or deductible in the Contracting State where such permanent establishment is situated, even if the payments are deferred until such permanent establishment or fixed base has ceased to exist.

ARTICLE 8

Shipping and Air Transport

1. Profits of an enterprise of a Contracting State from the operation in international traffic of ships or aircraft shall be taxable only in that State.

2. For purposes of this Article, profits from the operation in international traffic of ships or aircraft include profits derived from the rental on a full or bareboat basis of ships or aircraft if operated in international traffic by the lessee or if such rental profits are incidental to other profits described in paragraph 1.

3. Profits of an enterprise of a Contracting State from the rental or maintenance of containers (including trailers, barges and related equipment for the transport of containers) used in international traffic shall be taxable only in that State.

4. The provisions of paragraphs 1 and 3 shall also apply to profits derived from the participation in a pool, a joint business or an international operating agency.

ARTICLE 9

Associated Enterprises

1. Where

a) an enterprise of a Contracting State participates directly or indirectly in the management, control or capital of an enterprise of the other Contracting State, or

b) the same persons participate directly or indirectly in the management, control or capital of an enterprise of a Contracting State and an enterprise of the other Contracting State,

and in either case conditions are made or imposed between the two enterprises in their commercial or financial relations which differ from those which would be made between independent enterprises, then any profits which would, but for those conditions, have not so accrued, may be included in the profits of that enterprise and taxed accordingly.

2. Where a Contracting State includes in the profits of an enterprise of that State, and taxes accordingly, profits on which an enterprise of the other Contracting State has been charged to tax in that other State, and the profits so included are profits which would have accrued to the enterprise of the first-mentioned State if the conditions made between the two enterprises had been those which would have been made between independent enterprises, then that other State shall make an appropriate adjustment to the amount of the tax charged therein on those profits. In determining such adjustment, due regard shall be had to the other provisions of this Convention and the competent authorities of the Contracting States shall if necessary consult each other.

3. The provisions of paragraph 1 shall not limit any provisions of the law of either Contracting State which permit the distribution, apportionment or allocation of income, deductions, credits, or allowances between persons owned or controlled directly or indirectly by the same interests when necessary in order to prevent evasion of taxes or clearly to reflect the income of any of such persons.

ARTICLE 10
Dividends

1. Dividends paid by a company which is a resident of a Contracting State to a resident of the other Contracting State may be taxed by both Contracting States.

2. However, if the beneficial owner of the dividends is a resident of the other Contracting State, the tax charged in the first-mentioned Contracting State shall not exceed:

a) 10 percent of the gross amount of the dividends if the beneficial owner is a company which owns, directly or indirectly, at least 10 percent of the voting stock of the company paying the dividends;

  b) 15 percent of the gross amount of the dividends in all other cases.

The provisions of this paragraph shall not affect the taxation of the company in respect of the profits out of which the dividends are paid.

  3. Subparagraph a) of paragraph 2 shall not apply in the case of dividends paid by a United States Regulated Investment Company (RIC) or a Real Estate Investment Trust (REIT). In the case of dividends from a RIC, subparagraph b) of paragraph 2 shall apply. In the case of dividends paid by a REIT, subparagraph b) shall apply instead of the rate of tax applicable under domestic law only if:

  a) the beneficial owner of the dividends is an individual holding an interest of no more than 10 percent in the REIT;

  b) the dividends are paid with respect to a class of stock that is publicly traded and the beneficial owner of the dividends is a person holding an interest of no more than 5 percent in any class of the REIT's stock; or

  c) the beneficial owner of the dividends is a person that holds an interest of no more than 10 percent in the REIT and the REIT is diversified.

  4. The term "dividends" as used in this Convention means income from shares or other rights, not being debt-claims, participating in profits, as well as income from other corporate rights which is subjected to the same taxation treatment as income from shares by the taxation law of the State of which the company making the distribution is a resident, and income from arrangements, including debt obligations, carrying the right to participate in profits, to the extent so characterized under the laws of the Contracting State in which the income arises.

5. The provisions of paragraphs 1, 2 and 3 shall not apply if the beneficial owner of the dividends, being a resident of a Contracting State, carries on business in the other Contracting State, of which the company paying the dividends is a resident, through a permanent establishment situated therein, or performs in that other State independent personal services from a fixed base situated therein, and the holding in respect of which the dividends are paid is effectively connected with such permanent establishment or fixed base. In such a case, the provisions of Article 7 (Business Profits) or Article 15 (Independent Personal Services), as the case may be, shall apply.

ARTICLE 11

Interest

1. Interest derived by a resident of one of the Contracting States from sources within the other Contracting State may be taxed by both Contracting States.

2. Interest derived and beneficially owned by a resident of one of the Contracting States from sources within the other Contracting State shall not be taxed by the other Contracting State at a rate in excess of 10 percent of the gross amount of such interest.

3. Notwithstanding the provisions of paragraphs 1 and 2:

a) Interest derived by one of the Contracting States, or an instrumentality thereof (including the Bangladesh Bank, the Federal Reserve Banks of the United States, the Export-Import Bank of the United States, the Overseas Private Investment Corporation of the United States, and such other institutions of either Contracting State as the competent authorities of both Contracting States may determine by mutual agreement) from sources in the other Contracting State shall be exempt from tax by that other Contracting State. Interest on a debt obligation guaranteed or insured by one of the   Contracting States, or an instrumentality thereof, shall be exempt from tax by that State;

      b) Interest derived and beneficially owned by a bank or other financial institution (including an insurance company) that is a resident of a Contracting State from sources within the other Contracting State shall not be taxed by the other Contracting State at a rate in excess of 5 percent of the gross amount of the interest; and

      c) Interest derived and beneficially owned by a resident of a Contracting State from sources within the other Contracting State in connection with the sale on credit to an enterprise of the other Contracting State of any industrial, commercial or scientific equipment or of any merchandise, shall not be taxed by the other Contracting State at a rate in excess of 5 percent of the gross amount of the interest.

4. The provisions of paragraphs 2 and 3 shall not apply if the beneficial owner of interest from sources within one of the Contracting States, being a resident of the other Contracting State, carries on business in the first-mentioned Contracting State through a permanent establishment situated therein or performs in that other State independent personal services from a fixed base situated therein, and the debt-claim in respect of which the interest is paid is effectively connected with such permanent establishment or fixed base. In such a case, the provisions of Article 7 (Business Profits) or Article 15 (Independent Personal Services), as the case may be, shall apply.

5. Where an amount is paid to a related person and would be treated as interest but for the fact that it exceeds an amount which would have been paid to an unrelated person, the provisions of this Article shall apply only to so much of the amount as would have been paid to an unrelated person. In such a case, the

excess amount may be taxed by   each Contracting State according to its own laws, including the provisions of this Convention where applicable.

6. The term "interest" as used in this Convention means income from debt-claims of every kind, whether or not secured by mortgage, and whether or not carrying a right to participate in the debtor's profits, and in particular, income from government securities and income from bonds or debentures, including premiums and prizes attaching to such securities, bonds or debentures, and including an excess inclusion with respect to a residual interest in a real estate mortgage investment conduit, as well as income assimilated to income from money lent by the taxation law of the Contracting State in which the income arises, including interest on deferred payment sales. However, the term "interest" does not include income dealt with in Article 10 (Dividends).

7. The provisions of paragraphs 2 and 3 shall not apply to:

a) an excess inclusion with respect to a residual interest in a real estate mortgage investment conduit; such an interest may be taxed in the Contracting State where the excess inclusion arises according to the laws of that State; or

b) interest that is contingent interest of a type that does not qualify as portfolio interest under United States law, and to equivalent amounts under Bangladesh law; such interest may be taxed at a rate not exceeding the rate prescribed in subparagraph b) of paragraph 2 of Article 10 (Dividends).

8. Interest shall be deemed to arise from sources within a Contracting State when the payer is a resident of that State. Where, however, the person paying the interest, whether he is a resident of a Contracting State or not, has in a Contracting State a permanent establishment or a fixed base and such interest

is borne by such permanent   establishment or fixed base, then such interest shall be deemed to arise from sources within the State in which the permanent establishment or fixed base is situated.

ARTICLE 12
Royalties

1. Royalties derived by a resident of one of the Contracting States from sources within the other Contracting State may be taxed by both Contracting States.

2. Royalties derived and beneficially owned by a resident of one of the Contracting States from sources within the other Contracting State shall not be taxed by that other Contracting State at a rate in excess of 10 percent of the gross amount of such royalties.

3. The term "royalties" as used in this Article means payments of any kind received as a consideration for the use of, or the right to use, any copyright of literary, artistic or scientific work including cinematographic films or tapes used for radio or television broadcasting, and any patent, trademark, design or model, plan, secret formula or process, or other like right or property, or for information concerning industrial, commercial or scientific experience. The term "royalties" also includes gains derived from the alienation of any such right or property which are contingent on the productivity, use, or disposition thereof. However, the term "royalties" does not include any payments in consideration for the working of, or the right to work, mineral deposits, sources and other natural resources.

4. The provisions of paragraphs 1 and 2 shall not apply if the recipient of the royalties from sources within one of the Contracting States, being a resident of the other Contracting State, carries on business in the first-mentioned Contracting

State through a permanent   establishment situated therein, or performs in that other State independent personal services from a fixed base situated therein, and the right or property in respect of which the royalties are paid is effectively connected with such permanent establishment or fixed base. In such a case the provisions of Article 7 (Business Profits) or Article 15 (Independent Personal Services), as the case may be, shall apply.

5. Where an amount is paid to a related person and would be treated as a royalty but for the fact that it exceeds an amount which would have been paid to an unrelated person, the provisions of this Article shall apply only to so much of the amount as would have been paid to an unrelated person. In such case, the excess amount may be taxed by each Contracting State according to its own laws, including the provisions of this Convention where applicable.

6. Royalties shall be deemed to arise from sources within a Contracting State when they are in consideration for the use of, or the right to use, in that State, property or information concerning industrial, commercial or scientific experience.

ARTICLE 13

Capital Gains

1.   a) Gains derived by a resident of a Contracting State from the alienation of immovable property situated in the other Contracting State may be taxed in that other State;

b) For purposes of this paragraph the term "immovable property" means property referred to in Article 6 (Income From Immovable Property). When the United States is the other Contracting State described in subparagraph a), the term includes a United States real property interest. When Bangladesh is the other Contracting State described in subparagraph a), the term includes shares of the capital stock of a company the   property of which consists principally of immovable property situated in Bangladesh.

2. Gains from the alienation of movable property forming part of the business property of a permanent establishment which an enterprise of a Contracting State has in the other Contracting State or of movable property pertaining to a fixed base available to a resident of a Contracting State in the other Contracting State for the purpose of performing independent personal services, including such gains from the alienation of such a permanent establishment, alone or with the whole enterprise, or of such fixed base, may be taxed in that other State.

3. Gains derived by an enterprise of a Contracting State from the alienation of ships, aircraft or containers operated in international traffic shall be taxable only in that State, and gains described in Article 12 (Royalties) shall be taxable only in accordance with the provisions of Article 12.

4. Gains from the alienation of any property, other than that referred to in paragraphs 1, 2 and 3, shall be taxable only in the Contracting State of which the alienator is a resident.

ARTICLE 14

Branch Tax

1. A company which is a resident of a Contracting State may be subject in the other Contracting State to a tax in addition to the tax allowable under the other provisions of this Convention.

2. Such tax, however, may be imposed only on:

a) in the case of the United States:

i) the "dividend equivalent amount" of the business profits that are effectively connected (or treated as effectively connected) with the conduct of a trade or business in the United States and are either attributable to a permanent establishment in the United States or subject to tax in the United States on a net

basis under Article 6 (Income From Immovable Property)
or Article 13 (Capital Gains) of this Convention; and

ii) the excess, if any, of interest deductible in
the United States in computing the profits of the
company that are subject to tax in the United States
and are either attributable to a permanent
establishment in the United States or subject to tax in
the United States on a net basis under Article 6
(Income From Immovable Property) or Article 13 (Capital
Gains) of this Convention over the interest paid by or
from the permanent establishment or trade or business
in the United States.

b) in the case of Bangladesh, an amount sufficient to
provide that a branch in Bangladesh of a United States
company (or a company of the United States otherwise taxable
on net income in Bangladesh) is taxed in a manner comparable
to a similarly situated Bangladesh company and its United
States shareholder.

3. The taxes described in the preceding paragraphs shall not
be imposed at a rate exceeding:

a) the rate specified in paragraph 2a) of Article 10
(Dividends) for the taxes described in paragraphs 2a)i) and
2b) of this Article; and

b) the appropriate rate specified in paragraphs 2 or 3
of Article 11 (Interest) for the tax described in
subparagraph 2(a)(ii).

ARTICLE 15

Independent Personal Services

Income derived by an individual who is a resident of a
Contracting State from the performance of personal services in an
independent capacity shall be taxable only in that State unless
such services are performed in the other Contracting State and

a) the individual is present in that other State for a period or periods exceeding in the aggregate 183 days in any 12-month period commencing or ending in the income year or taxable year concerned; or

b) the individual has a fixed base regularly available to him in that other State for the purpose of performing his activities, but only so much of the income as is attributable to that fixed base may be taxed in such other State.

ARTICLE 16

Dependent Personal Services

1. Subject to the provisions of Articles 18 (Entertainers and Athletes), 19 (Pensions, Et Cetera), 20 (Government Service) and 21 (Teachers, Students and Trainees), salaries, wages and other remuneration derived by a resident of a Contracting State in respect of an employment shall be taxable only in that State unless the employment is exercised in the other Contracting State. If the employment is so exercised, such remuneration as is derived therefrom may be taxed in that other State.

2. Notwithstanding the provisions of paragraph 1, remuneration derived by a resident of a Contracting State in respect of an employment exercised in the other Contracting State shall be taxable only in the first-mentioned State if:

a) the recipient is present in the other State for a period or periods not exceeding in the aggregate 183 days in any 12-month period commencing or ending in the income year or taxable year concerned;

b) the remuneration is paid by, or on behalf of, an employer who is not a resident of the other State; and

c) the remuneration is not borne by a permanent establishment or a fixed base which the employer has in the other State.

3. Notwithstanding the   preceding provisions of this
Article, remuneration described in paragraph 1 derived in respect
of an employment as a member of the regular complement of a ship
or aircraft operated by an enterprise of a Contracting State in
international traffic may be taxed only in that Contracting
State.

4. Notwithstanding the other provisions of this Article and
Article 15 (Independent Personal Services), where a director's
fee is paid by a company which is a resident of a Contracting
State to an individual who is a resident of the other Contracting
State and is a shareholder of the company, and such fee is in
excess of the amount which would have been paid for such services
to an individual who is not a shareholder of the company, such
excess amount may be taxed by the first-mentioned Contracting
State at a rate not in excess of 15 percent.

ARTICLE 17
Limitation on Benefits

1. A person which is a resident of a Contracting State and
derives income from the other Contracting State shall be
entitled, in that other Contracting State, to all the benefits of
this Convention only if such person is:

a) an individual;

b) a Contracting State or a political subdivision or
local authority thereof;

c) a person, if:

i) more than 50 percent of the beneficial interest
in such person (or in the case of a company, more than
50 percent of the number of shares of each class of the
company's shares) is owned, directly or indirectly, by
persons entitled to benefits of this Convention under
subparagraphs a), b), d), e) or f) of this paragraph or

who are citizens of the United States; and

ii) not more than 50 percent of the gross income
of such person is used, directly or indirectly, to make
deductible payments (including payments of interest or
royalties) to persons who are not entitled to benefits
of this Convention under subparagraph a), b), d), e) or
f) of this paragraph and are not citizens of the United
States;

d) a company in whose principal class of shares there
is substantial and regular trading on a recognized stock
exchange;

e) a company in which at least 50 percent of each class
of shares in the company is owned directly or indirectly by
five or fewer companies entitled to benefits under
subparagraph d), provided that in the case of indirect
ownership, each intermediate owner is a person entitled to
the benefits of the Convention under this paragraph; or

f) an entity which is a not-for-profit organization as
described in subparagraph c) of paragraph 1 of Article 4
(Fiscal Domicile), provided that, with respect to entities
described in clause ii) of that paragraph, more than half of
the beneficiaries, members or participants, if any, in such
organization are persons that are entitled, under this
Article, to the benefits of the Convention.

2. a) A resident of a Contracting State will be
entitled to benefits of the Convention with respect to an
item of income derived from the other State, regardless of
whether the resident is qualified for benefits under
paragraph 1 of this Article, if the resident is engaged in
the active conduct of a trade or business in the first-
mentioned State (other than the business of making or
managing investments for the resident's own account, unless
these activities are banking, insurance or securities

activities carried on by a bank, insurance company or registered securities dealer) and the income derived from the other Contracting State is derived in connection with, or is incidental to, that trade or business.

b) If the resident or any of its associated enterprises has an ownership interest in the activity in the other Contracting State from which the item of income is derived, the rule of subparagraph a) shall apply only if the trade or business in the first-mentioned State is substantial in relation to the activity in the other State. Whether a trade or business is substantial for purposes of this paragraph will be determined on the basis of all the facts and circumstances.

c) Income is derived "in connection with" a trade or business when the activity in the other State generating the income is a line of business that forms a part of or is complementary to the trade or business. Income is "incidental to" a trade or business when it facilitates the conduct of the trade or business in the other State.

3. A person that is not entitled to the benefits of the Convention pursuant to the provisions of paragraph 1 or 2 may, nevertheless, be granted the benefits of the Convention if the competent authority of the Contracting State in which the income in question arises so determines.

4. For purposes of subparagraph d) of paragraph 1, the term "a recognized stock exchange" means:

a) the NASDAQ System owned by the National Association of Securities Dealers, Inc. and any stock exchange registered with the U.S. Securities and Exchange Commission as a national securities exchange for purposes of the U.S. Securities Exchange Act of 1934;

b) the stock exchanges regulated by the Bangladesh Securities and Exchange Commission; and

c) any other stock   exchange agreed upon by the competent authorities of the Contracting States.

5. The competent authorities of the Contracting States may consult together with a view to developing procedures for the application of the provisions of this Article. The competent authorities shall, in accordance with the provisions of Article 26 (Exchange of Information and Administrative Assistance), exchange such information as is necessary for carrying out the provisions of this Article and safeguarding, in cases envisioned therein, the application of their domestic law.

ARTICLE 18

Entertainers and Athletes

1. Notwithstanding the provisions of Articles 15 (Independent Personal Services) and 16 (Dependent Personal Services), income derived by public entertainers such as theater, motion picture, radio or television artistes, and musicians, and by athletes, from their personal activities as such may be taxed in the Contracting State in which these activities are exercised provided that such income exceeds in the aggregate 10,000 United States dollars or its equivalent in Bangladesh taka during the income year or taxable year. However, such income shall not be taxable in such Contracting State if the income is derived from activities exercised in that Contracting State by a resident of the other Contracting State as an entertainer or athlete and the visit to the first-mentioned State is wholly or mainly supported by public funds of the other State or a political subdivision or local authority thereof.

2. Where income in respect of activities exercised by an entertainer or an athlete in his capacity as such accrues not to that entertainer or athlete but to another person, that income may, notwithstanding the provisions of Articles 7 (Business Profits), 15 (Independent Personal Services), and 16 (Dependent

Personal Services), be taxed in the Contracting State in which the activities of the entertainer or athlete are exercised. For purposes of the preceding sentence, income of an entertainer or athlete shall be deemed not to accrue to another person if it is established that neither the entertainer or athlete, nor persons related thereto, participate directly or indirectly in the profits of such other person in any manner, including the receipt of deferred remuneration, bonuses, fees, dividends, partnership distributions or other distributions.

ARTICLE 19

Pensions, Et Cetera

1. Subject to the provisions of paragraph 2 of Article 20 (Government Service), pensions and other similar remuneration beneficially derived by a resident of a Contracting State, whether paid periodically or as a single sum, in consideration of past employment shall be taxable only in that State.

2. Social security payments and other public pensions paid by a Contracting State to an individual who is a resident of the other Contracting State or a citizen of the United States shall be taxable only in the first-mentioned Contracting State.

3. Annuities beneficially derived by a resident of a Contracting State shall be taxable only in that State. The term "annuities" as used in this paragraph means a stated sum paid periodically at stated times during life or during a specified number of years, under an obligation to make the payments in return for adequate and full consideration (other than services rendered).

4. Alimony paid to a resident of a Contracting State by a resident of the other Contracting State shall be exempt from tax in the other Contracting State. The term "alimony" as used in this paragraph means periodic payments made pursuant to a written separation agreement or a decree of divorce, separate

maintenance, or compulsory   support, which payments are taxable to the recipient under the laws of the State of which he is a resident.

5. Periodic payments not dealt with in paragraph 4 for the support of a minor child made pursuant to a written separation agreement or a decree of divorce, separate maintenance, or compulsory support, paid by a resident of one of the Contracting States to a resident of the other Contracting State, shall be exempt from tax in both Contracting States.

ARTICLE 20
Government Service

1.   a) Remuneration, other than a pension, paid by a Contracting State or a political subdivision or a local authority thereof to any individual in respect of services rendered to that State or subdivision or authority shall be taxable only in that State.

b) However, such remuneration shall be taxable only in the other Contracting State if the services are rendered in that other State and the individual is a resident of that State who:

i) is a national of that State; or

ii) did not become a resident of that State solely for the purpose of rendering the services.

2. Subject to the provisions of paragraph 2 of Article 19 (Pensions, Et Cetera):

a) Any pension paid by, or out of funds created by, a Contracting State or a political subdivision or local authority thereof to an individual in respect of services rendered to that State or subdivision or authority shall be taxable only in that State.

b) However, such   pension shall be taxable only in the other Contracting State if the individual is a resident of, and a national of, that State.

3. The provisions of Articles 15 (Independent Personal Services), 16 (Dependent Personal Services), 18 (Entertainers and Athletes), and 19 (Pensions, Et Cetera), as the case may be, shall apply to remuneration and pensions in respect of services rendered in connection with a business carried on by a Contracting State or a political subdivision or a local authority thereof.

ARTICLE 21
Teachers, Students and Trainees

1. An individual who visits temporarily one of the Contracting States for the purpose of teaching or engaging in research at a university, college or other recognized educational institution in that Contracting State, and who was immediately before that visit a resident of the other Contracting State, shall be exempt from tax in the first-mentioned Contracting State on any remuneration for such teaching or research for a period not exceeding two years from the date he first visits that State for such purpose.

2. An individual who was a resident of a Contracting State immediately before visiting the other Contracting State and is temporarily present in that other State for the primary purpose of:

a) studying at a university, college, school or other recognized educational institution in that other State;

b) securing training as a business or technical apprentice; or

c) studying or doing research as a recipient of a grant allowance or award from a governmental, religious, charitable, or educational organization;

shall, from the date of his first arrival in that other State in connection with that visit, be exempt from tax in that other State with respect to:

> i) all remittances from abroad for purposes of his maintenance, education or training;

> ii) the grant, allowance, or award; and

> iii) any remuneration for personal services rendered in that other Contracting State with a view to supplementing the resources available to him for such purposes in an amount not in excess of 8,000 United States dollars or its equivalent in Bangladesh taka for any taxable year.

In the case of an individual described in subparagraph b), this exemption from tax shall apply for a period not exceeding two years from the date of the individual's first arrival in the other State.

3. This Article shall not apply to income from research if such research is undertaken not in the public interest but primarily for the private benefit of a specific person or persons.

ARTICLE 22

Other Income

1. Items of income of a resident of a Contracting State, wherever arising, not dealt with in the foregoing Articles of this Convention shall be taxable only in that State.

2. The provisions of paragraph 1 shall not apply to income, other than income from immovable property as defined in paragraph 2 of Article 6 (Income From Immovable Property) if the recipient of such income, being a resident of a Contracting State, carries on business in the other Contracting State through a permanent establishment situated therein, or performs in that other State independent personal services from a fixed base situated therein,

and the right or property in   respect of which the income is
paid is effectively connected with such permanent establishment
or fixed base. In such case the provisions of Article 7
(Business Profits) or Article 15 (Independent Personal Services),
as the case may be, shall apply.

3. Notwithstanding paragraphs 1 and 2, items of income of a
resident of a Contracting State not dealt with in the foregoing
Articles of this Convention and arising in the other Contracting
State may be taxed in that other State.

ARTICLE 23
Relief From Double Taxation

1. In accordance with the provisions and subject to the
limitations of the law of the United States (as it may be amended
from time to time without changing the general principle hereof),
the United States shall allow to a resident or citizen of the
United States as a credit against the United States tax on income
the appropriate amount of tax paid or accrued to Bangladesh by or
on behalf of such citizen or resident; and, in the case of a
United States company owning at least 10 percent of the voting
stock of a company which is a resident of Bangladesh from which
the United States company receives a dividend in any taxable
year, the United States shall allow a credit for the appropriate
amount of tax paid or accrued to Bangladesh by or on behalf of
the payor with respect to the profits out of which such dividends
are paid. Such appropriate amount shall be based upon the amount
of tax paid or accrued to Bangladesh, but the credit shall not
exceed the limitations (for the purpose of limiting the credit to
the United States tax on income from sources outside the United
States) provided by United States law for the taxable year. For
purposes of applying the United States credit in relation to tax
paid to Bangladesh, the taxes referred to in paragraphs 2(b) and

3 of Article 2 (Taxes Covered) shall be considered to be income taxes.

2. In accordance with the provisions and subject to the limitations of the law of Bangladesh (as it may be amended from time to time without changing the general principle hereof), Bangladesh shall allow a resident of Bangladesh as a credit against the Bangladesh tax the appropriate amount of tax paid or accrued to the United States by or on behalf of such resident or citizen; and, in the case of a Bangladesh company owning at least 10 percent of the voting stock of a company which is a resident of the United States from which it receives a dividend in any income year, Bangladesh shall allow a credit for the appropriate amount of tax paid or accrued to the United States by that company with respect to the profits out of which such dividends are paid. Such appropriate amount shall be based upon the amount of tax paid or accrued to the United States, but the credit shall not exceed the limitations (for the purpose of limiting the credit to the Bangladesh tax on income from sources outside of Bangladesh) provided by Bangladesh law for the income year. For purposes of applying the Bangladesh credit in relation to tax paid to the United States, the taxes referred to in paragraphs 2(a) and 3 of Article 2 (Taxes Covered) shall be considered to be income taxes.

3. Where a United States citizen is a resident of Bangladesh:

a) with respect to items of income that under the provisions of this Convention are exempt from United States tax or that are subject to a reduced rate of United States tax when derived by a resident of Bangladesh who is not a United States citizen, Bangladesh shall allow as a credit against Bangladesh tax only the tax paid, if any, that the United States may impose under the provisions of this Convention, other than taxes that may be imposed solely by reason of citizenship under the saving clause of paragraph 2 of Article 1 (Personal Scope);

b) for purposes of computing United States tax on those items of income referred to in subparagraph a), the United States shall allow as a credit against United States tax the income tax paid to Bangladesh after the credit referred to in subparagraph a); the credit so allowed shall not reduce the portion of the United States tax that is creditable against the Bangladesh tax in accordance with subparagraph a); and

c) for the exclusive purpose of relieving double taxation in the United States under subparagraph b), items referred to in subparagraph a) shall be deemed to arise in Bangladesh to the extent necessary to avoid double taxation of such income under subparagraph b).

ARTICLE 24

Nondiscrimination

1. Nationals of a Contracting State shall not be subjected in the other State to any taxation or any requirement connected therewith which is other or more burdensome than the taxation and connected requirements to which nationals of that other State in the same circumstances are or may be subjected. For purposes of United States taxation, United States nationals who are not resident in the United States are not in the same circumstances as Bangladesh nationals who are not resident in the United States. This provision shall, notwithstanding the provisions of Article 1 (Personal Scope), also apply to persons who are not residents of either Contracting State.

2. The taxation on a permanent establishment or a fixed base which a resident or enterprise of a Contracting State has in the other Contracting State shall not be less favorably levied in

that other State than the   taxation levied on residents or enterprises of that other State carrying on the same activities.

3. Except where the provisions of paragraph 1 of Article 9 (Associated Enterprises), paragraph 5 of Article 11 (Interest), or paragraph 5 of Article 12 (Royalties) apply, interest, royalties and other disbursements paid by an enterprise of a Contracting State to a resident of the other Contracting State shall, for the purpose of determining the taxable profits of such enterprise, be deductible under the same conditions as if they had been paid to a resident of the first-mentioned State. The provisions of this paragraph shall not affect the application of the law of Bangladesh requiring the deduction of tax at source, from interest, royalties and other disbursements as a condition for deduction. Any debts of a resident of a Contracting State to a resident of the other Contracting State shall, for the purpose of determining the taxable capital of the first-mentioned resident, be deductible under the same conditions as if they had been contracted to a resident of the first-mentioned State.

4. Enterprises of a Contracting State, the capital of which is wholly or partly owned or controlled, directly or indirectly, by one or more residents of the other Contracting State, shall not be subjected in the first-mentioned State to any taxation or any requirement connected therewith which is other or more burdensome than the taxation and connected requirements to which other similar enterprises of the first-mentioned State are or may be subjected.

5. Nothing in this Article shall be construed as obliging a Contracting State to grant to residents of the other Contracting State any personal allowances, reliefs and reductions for taxation purposes which it grants to its own residents.

6. Nothing in this Article shall be construed as preventing either Contracting State from imposing the tax described in Article 14 (Branch Tax).

7. The provisions of this Article shall apply to taxes of every kind and description imposed by a Contracting State or a political subdivision or local authority thereof.

ARTICLE 25

Mutual Agreement Procedure

1. Where a person considers that the actions of one or both of the Contracting States result or will result for him in taxation not in accordance with the provisions of this Convention, he may, irrespective of the remedies provided by the domestic law of those States, and the time limits prescribed in such laws for presenting claims for a refund, present his case to the competent authority of either Contracting State.

2. The competent authority shall endeavor, if the objection appears to it to be justified and if it is not itself able to arrive at a satisfactory solution, to resolve the case by mutual agreement with the competent authority of the other Contracting State, with a view to the avoidance of taxation which is not in accordance with the Convention. If an agreement is reached, it shall be implemented notwithstanding any time limits in the domestic law of the Contracting States. Assessment and collection procedures shall be suspended during the pendency of any mutual agreement proceeding.

3. The competent authorities of the Contracting States shall endeavor to resolve by mutual agreement any difficulties or doubts arising as to the interpretation or application of the Convention. In particular the competent authorities of the Contracting States may agree:

> a) to the same attribution of income, deductions, credits, or allowances of an enterprise of a Contracting State to its permanent establishment situated in the other Contracting State;

> b) to the same allocation of income, deductions, credits, or allowances between persons, including a uniform position on the application of the requirements of paragraph 2 of Article 24 (Nondiscrimination);

c) to the same   characterization of particular items of income;

d) to the same application of source rules with respect to particular items of income; and

e) to a common meaning of a term.

They may also consult together for the elimination of double taxation in cases not provided for in the Convention.

4. The competent authorities of the Contracting States may communicate with each other directly for the purpose of reaching an agreement in the sense of the preceding paragraphs.

5. In cases where this Convention specifies a dollar amount, the competent authorities may agree to a higher dollar amount.

ARTICLE 26
Exchange of Information and
Administrative Assistance

1. The competent authorities of the Contracting States shall exchange such information as is necessary for carrying out the provisions of this Convention or of the domestic laws of the Contracting States concerning taxes covered by the Convention insofar as the taxation thereunder is not contrary to the Convention. The exchange of information is not restricted by Article 1 (Personal Scope). Any information received by a Contracting State shall be treated as secret in the same manner as information obtained under the domestic laws of that State and shall be disclosed only to persons or authorities, including court and administrative bodies, involved in the assessment, collection or administration of, the enforcement or prosecution in respect of, or the determination of appeals in relation to, the taxes covered by the Convention, or the oversight of the above. Such persons or authorities shall use the information only for the purposes described above. They may disclose the

information for such purposes in public court proceedings or in judicial decisions.

2. In no case shall the provisions of paragraph 1 be construed so as to impose on a Contracting State the obligation:

    a) to carry out administrative measures at variance with the laws and administrative practice of that or of the other Contracting State;

    b) to supply information which is not obtainable under the laws or in the normal course of the administration of that or of the other Contracting State;

    c) to supply information which would disclose any trade, business, industrial, commercial or professional secret or trade process, or information the disclosure of which would be contrary to public policy (ordre public).

3. Notwithstanding paragraph 2, the competent authority of the requested State shall, in accordance with paragraph 1,

    a) obtain and provide information held by financial institutions, nominees or persons acting in an agency or fiduciary capacity (not including information that would reveal confidential communications between a client and an attorney, solicitor or other legal representative, where the client seeks legal advice), or respecting interests in a person; and

    b) obtain and provide information requested by a Contracting State in accordance with this Article even if it does not need, for its own tax purposes, the information requested.

4. If specifically requested by the competent authority of a Contracting State, the competent authority of the other Contracting State shall provide information under this Article in the form of depositions of witnesses and authenticated copies of unedited original documents (including books, papers, statements, records, accounts and writings), to the extent such depositions

and documents can be obtained   under the laws and
administrative practices of that other State with respect to its
own taxes.

ARTICLE 27

Effect of Convention on Diplomatic Agents and Consular
Officers, Domestic Laws, And Other Treaties

1. Nothing in this Convention shall affect the fiscal
privileges of diplomatic agents or consular officers under the
general rules of international law or under the provisions of
special agreements.

2. This Convention shall not restrict in any manner any
exclusion, exemption, deduction, credit, or other allowance now
or hereafter accorded:

      a) by the laws of either Contracting State, or

      b) by any other agreement between the Contracting
States.

3. a) Notwithstanding the provisions of subparagraph 2b):

      i) the provisions of Article 25 (Mutual Agreement
Procedure) of this Convention exclusively shall apply
to any dispute concerning whether a measure is within
the scope of this Convention, and the procedures under
this Convention exclusively shall apply to that
dispute; and

      ii) unless the competent authorities determine
that a taxation measure is not within the scope of this
Convention, the nondiscrimination obligations of this
Convention exclusively shall apply with respect to that
measure, except for such national treatment or most-
favored-nation obligations as may apply to trade in
goods under the General Agreement on Tariffs and Trade.
No national treatment or most-favored-nation
obligation under any other agreement shall apply with

respect to that   measure.

b) For the purpose of this paragraph, a "measure" is a law, regulation, rule, procedure, decision, administrative action, or any similar provision or action.

ARTICLE 28
Entry Into Force

1. This Convention shall be subject to ratification in accordance with the applicable procedures of each Contracting State and instruments of ratification shall be exchanged as soon as possible.

2. The Convention shall enter into force upon the exchange of instruments of ratification and its provisions shall have effect:

a) in respect of taxes withheld at source, to amounts paid or credited on or after the first day of the second month next following the date on which this Convention enters into force; and

b) in respect of other taxes, to taxable periods in the United States and income years in Bangladesh beginning on or after the first day of January next following the date on which this Convention enters into force.

ARTICLE 29
Termination

This Convention shall remain in force until terminated by one of the Contracting States. Either Contracting State may terminate the Convention at any time after 5 years from the date on which this Convention enters into force, provided that at least 6 months' prior notice of termination has been given to the other Contracting State through diplomatic channels. In such event, the Convention shall cease to have effect:

a) in respect of taxes withheld at source, to amounts paid or credited on or after the first day of January next following the expiration of the 6 month period; and

b) in respect of other taxes, to taxable periods in the United States and income years in Bangladesh beginning on or after the first day of January next following the expiration of the 6 month period.

IN WITNESS WHEREOF the undersigned, being duly authorized by their respective Governments, have signed this Convention.

DONE at Dhaka, in duplicate, this 26th day of September, 2004.

FOR THE GOVERNMENT OF THE   FOR THE GOVERNMENT OF THE
UNITED STATES OF AMERICA: PEOPLE'S REPUBLIC OF BANGLADESH:

www.ingramcontent.com/pod-product-compliance
Lightning Source LLC
Chambersburg PA
CBHW080629290526
45790CB00007B/2981